First Peoples
of the Arctic

Unangan of
the Aleutian Islands

Inuit of Greenland and Canada

Sami of Sapmi

TRISHA SERTORI

MACMILLAN

LIBRARY

First published in 2009 by
MACMILLAN EDUCATION AUSTRALIA PTY LTD
15–19 Claremont Street, South Yarra 3141

Visit our website at www.macmillan.com.au or go directly to www.macmillanlibrary.com.au

Associated companies and representatives throughout the world.

National Library of Australia Cataloguing-in-Publication entry

Sertori, Trisha.
    Of the Arctic: Unangan of Aleutian Islands, Inuit of Canada and Greenland, Sami of Sapmi / Trisha Sertori.

    ISBN 978 1 4202 6797 6 (hbk.)
    Sertori, Trisha. First peoples.
    Includes index.
    For primary school age.
    Arctic peoples - Juvenile literature.
    Aleuts - Juvenile literature.
    Eskimos - Juvenile literature.
    Inuit - Juvenile literature.
    Sami (European people) - Juvenile literature.

306.09113

Edited by Anna Fern
Text design by Stella Vassiliou and Cristina Neri, Canary Graphic Design
Cover design by Stella Vassiliou and Cristina Neri, Canary Graphic Design
Page layout by Cristina Neri, Canary Graphic Design
Photo research by Legend Images
Maps by Laurie Whiddon, Map Illustrations

Printed in China

Acknowledgements
Front cover photographs: Sami (Lap Tribe) Finland Rovaniemi Traditional Costumes, photo courtesy of JTB
Photo/Photolibrary, **top left**; Alaskan Native Aleut Women Weave Grass Basket, photo courtesy of Photolibrary/
AlaskaStock, **top right**; Inuit teens throat singing wearing their traditional clothing MR Pond Inlet Baffin Island
High Arctic Canada isol, photo © Visual & Written SL/Alamy/Photolibrary, **bottom**.

Background image courtesy of Istockphoto/© Alexander Hafemann.

Photos courtesy of:
Hulton Archives/Getty Images, **20**; Michael Melford/Getty Images, **6 (left)**; Sissie Brimberg/National
Geographic/Getty Images, **24**; National Geographic Stock/George Mobley, **22, 28**; © Bryan & Cherry Alexander
Photography/Alamy/Photolibrary, **16**; © infocusphotos.com/Alamy/Photolibrary, **29**; © Anders Ryman/Alamy/
Photolibrary, **25, 26**; © tbkmedia.de/Alamy/Photolibrary, **27**; © Visual & Written SL/Alamy/Photolibrary, **18**;
Alaska Stock/Photolibrary, **7, 8, 9, 10, 11, 13, 17, 19, 21**; JTB Photo/Photo Library, **4, 23**; Photo Researchers/
Photolibrary, **15, 30**; Shutterstock, **14**; Archives, Alaska and Polar Regions Collections, Rasmuson Library,
University of Alaska Fairbanks, **12**.

While every care has been taken to trace and acknowledge copyright, the publisher tenders their apologies
for any accidental infringement where copyright has proved untraceable. Where the attempt has been
unsuccessful, the publisher welcomes information that would redress the situation.

Internet addresses
At the time of printing, the Internet addresses appearing in this book were correct. Owing to the dynamic
nature of the Internet, however, we cannot guarantee that all these addresses will remain correct.

Contents

Glossary words

When a word is printed in **bold**, you can look up its meaning in the Glossary on page 31.

First peoples of the world

First peoples are the original inhabitants of a region. They have developed their own **culture**, traditions, laws and way of life over thousands of years. First peoples are also called **indigenous people**.

Today, there are more than 370 million indigenous people living all around the world, from the icy Arctic Circle to the deserts of Australia. Many indigenous cultures, however, have been damaged or destroyed by **colonists** who have moved onto indigenous peoples' lands.

This book will introduce you to some first peoples of the world. You will discover their history, how they live, and how they have survived in a changing world.

"The United Nations says"

"Indigenous peoples have suffered from historic injustices as a result of the **colonisation** and **dispossession** of their lands, territories and **resources**. The **United Nations** Declaration on the Rights of Indigenous Peoples recognises the urgent need to respect and promote the rights of indigenous peoples and their lands, territories and resources.

Adapted from the United Nations Declaration on the Rights of Indigenous Peoples, 2007

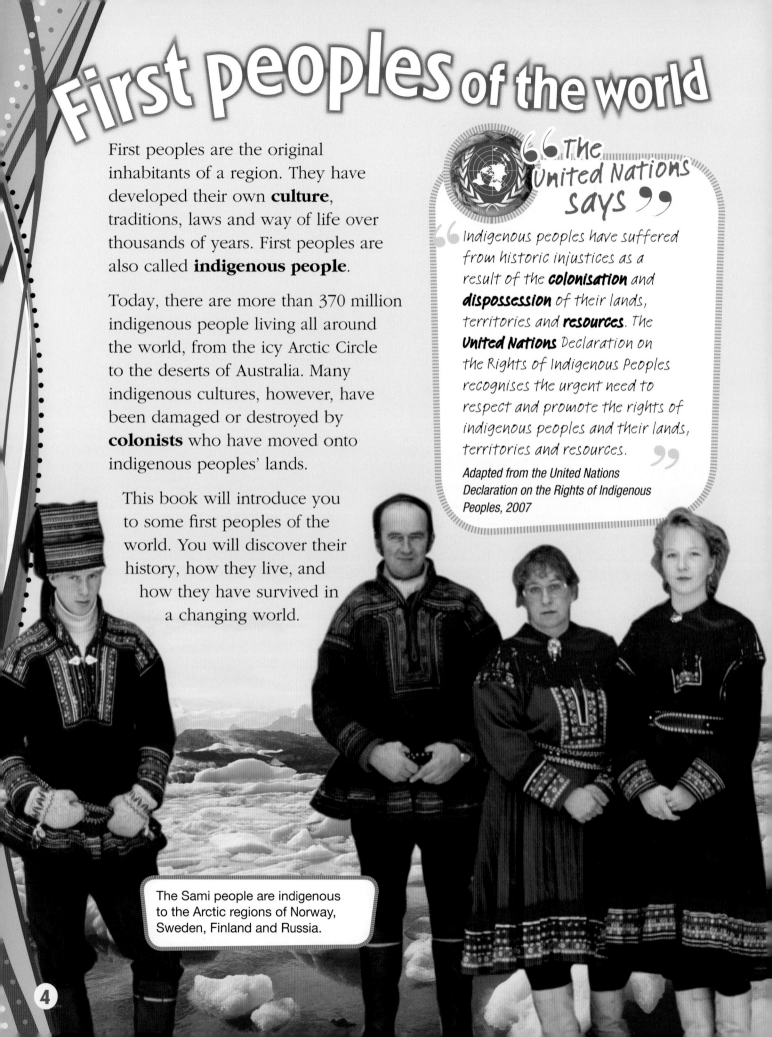

The Sami people are indigenous to the Arctic regions of Norway, Sweden, Finland and Russia.

First peoples of the Arctic

First peoples have lived on the edge of the Arctic Circle, near the North Pole, for thousands of years. In this book, we will meet:

- the Unangan people, from the Aleutian Islands
- the Inuit people, from Greenland and Canada
- the Sami people, from Norway, Sweden, Finland and Russia.

The region

The Arctic region includes northern Europe, Russia, Canada, Alaska, the Aleutian Islands, Iceland and Greenland.

Climate

The Arctic region is under ice for much of the year. Average winter temperatures are from minus 33 to minus 7 degrees Celsius. Average summer temperatures rise to 20 degrees Celsius. Some parts of the Arctic are permanently under ice, such as Greenland, the North Pole and parts of Alaska.

In winter, the sun is up for three to seven hours a day. In the summer months, the days are long, with 17 hours or more of daylight.

Did you know?

Scientists believe some Arctic peoples **migrated** from Asia to the Arctic across an ancient land bridge on the Bering Strait.

You can find out more information about the first peoples of the Arctic at www.alaskanative.net

The Unangan live on the Aleutian Islands in the Bering Strait. Unangan have lived continuously on this 1800-kilometre chain of islands for at least 9000 years.

The region

The Aleutian Islands are part of the United States. The main Aleutian city is Unalaska, on Unalaska Island in the Fox Islands.

The Aleutian islands are volcanic and rugged. The Aleutians are also treeless, freezing cold and windy.

The Aleutians are considered warm compared to other parts of the Arctic. In winter, temperatures range from minus 33 to minus 7 degrees Celsius. In summer, the temperature rises to 20 degrees Celsius.

Population

Today, 13 Unangan tribes live in ten villages on the main Aleutian Islands. The total Unangan population is around 8000.

Language

The language of the Aleutian Islands is Unangam Tunuu. Many Unangan speak their traditional language and English.

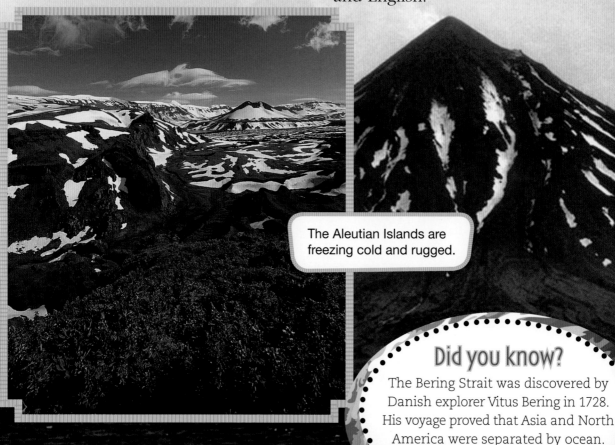

The Aleutian Islands are freezing cold and rugged.

Did you know?

The Bering Strait was discovered by Danish explorer Vitus Bering in 1728. His voyage proved that Asia and North America were separated by ocean.

Traditional dancers wear clothing decorated with feathers and fur.

Traditional Unangan life

Unangan people depended on the sea. Sea animals supplied food, as well as oil for fuel, and materials for clothing and canoes. Many Unangan now work for **commercial fisheries**.

Food and hunting

Women gathered roots, berries and rye grasses.

Men hunted in one-man canoes, called *baidarkas*, which were stable and fast in rough, freezing waters. Canoe frames of whalebone and **driftwood**, were covered with sealskin.

Housing

Early Unangan houses, called *ulax*, were dug into the ground. A driftwood or whalebone frame formed the roof and upper walls. Sods of earth were packed over the frame. Ulax were warm and housed several families. Today, Unangan live in modern brick or timber houses.

Clothing

Traditional full-length parkas were made from seal and fox fur and decorated with feathers, ivory and animal **sinew**. Shoes were made of animal hide. Today, most Unangan people wear jeans and nylon parkas.

Unangan society

Anthropologists believe that before colonisation around 25 000 Unangan people lived on the main Aleutian Islands.

Village social structure

Traditionally, villages were made up of extended families and slaves. Families worked together to hunt and gather food. Food was shared with all members of the community.

The heads of Unangan villages came from high-ranking families. They were selected for their wisdom and hunting ability. Village heads protected local fishing grounds. A special priest, called a shaman, carried out **rituals** to protect the community.

Today, Unangan are governed by village councils and corporations. Village councils are made up of tribal members. Village corporations manage Unangan land and resources.

Millie McKeown-Chuluulux

Millie McKeown-Chuluulux is an Unangan from the Aleutian Pribilof Islands. Millie says:

66 *The Village Council President represents the tribal members regarding issues of tribal sovereignty, tribal benefits and government relations.* 99

Unangan hunt in baidarkas in the freezing Bering Strait waters and share their catch with their community.

Traditionally, elders taught children life skills, such as hunting with spears.

Did you know?

Unangan games teach stamina and endurance. In the ear pull, players are bound together by animal sinew wound around their ear. Players pull backwards, and the winner is the one who can bear the pain longest.

Unangan learning for life

Traditionally, Unangan boys and girls were taught by their **elders**.

Learning traditional skills

Sea hunting was the most important job for Unangan men. At eight years of age, boys began learning to read the sea, sail baidarka, and fish and trap animals. They learned to sit for long periods with their legs out straight, to train for many hours at sea in their baidarka.

Girls learned to make the covering for baidarka from seal pelts. They learned to use animal intestines on seams to make fur clothing waterproof. Girls also learned to embroider clothing and weave grasses into baskets.

Modern education

Today, Unangan village schools follow the United States school curriculum. Unangan boys and girls also learn their traditional language and culture.

Unangan celebrations and rituals

Unangan weddings, games and feasts were held in the community hall, called a *qasgiq*, during winter. During celebrations, Unangan feasted on food that had been gathered and stored during summer.

Births

In Unangan society, special rituals were carried out to protect mothers and babies during birth. Babies were raised by older women while their mothers continued to gather foods and sew skins for baidarkas.

Marriages

Unangan communities are made up of loosely related family groups. Often, an Unangan would marry into the most distant family branch. Unangan men and women traditionally chose partners from their mother's cousin's line. Sometimes Unangan marriages had more than one husband or wife.

Funeral rites

Rituals for the dead lasted 40 days and ended with a feast. The deceased was buried with their hunting tools so they could hunt in the afterlife.

Did you know?

Unangan mummified or preserved the bodies of the deceased and laid them to rest in a sitting position.

Elaborate clothing, dancing and singing are part of many Unangan rituals.

Unangan arts and crafts

Weaving, embroidery and carving are the main traditional crafts of the Unangan people. Today many Unangan learn these skills at village community centres to preserve Unangan culture.

Basketry

Baskets made from rye grass have **geometric patterns** woven into them. There can be 1300 stitches per centimetre in the baskets, making Unangan baskets among the finest in the world.

Embroidery

Fur-lined parkas were embroidered with hair and wool. Parkas were also decorated with animal skin, feathers and ivory carvings.

Carving

Unangan men carved and painted masks used in rituals and celebrations. Visors to shield the eyes from the glare of the ice were also carved, painted and decorated with glass beads. Men carved walrus tusk ivory into **amulets**, fish hooks and animals.

Did you know?

A skilled hunter's visor was longer and more richly decorated than others.

Songs and storytelling

The cold months were the time for storytelling and songs. Many of these songs are still taught to young Unangan.

Unangan women weave baskets from grass.

Changes to Unangan life

The Unangan lived **sustainably** in the Arctic region for 9000 years by sharing their resources. Their way of life changed with colonisation. From 1740 to 1900, the Unangan population fell dramatically to around 4000 people. This was due to introduced diseases, malnutrition and forced relocation.

Russian colonisation

In the 1760s, Russia colonised the Aleutian Islands. Unangan hunted seals for Russian fur traders. In the 1800s, Russia declared the Unangan to be Russian **citizens** with the same rights and wages as other Russians.

American colonialism

In 1867, Russia sold Alaska and the Aleutian Islands to the United States. During World War II, the United States set up military bases on the Aleutian Islands. Unangan were placed in camps on the Alaskan mainland. Their homes were destroyed and **artefacts** stolen. Many Unangan traditions disappeared during this time.

" The United Nations says "

" Indigenous peoples shall not be forcibly removed from their lands or territories. "

Article 10 of the United Nations Declaration on the Rights of Indigenous Peoples, 2007

Unangan fleets hunted fur seals for Russian traders.

Unangan survival

Unangan have survived damage to their culture by colonialism. Today they are rebuilding their cultural traditions.

Education

Elders are again handing down to the young traditional skills once needed to live in the harsh Arctic Circle environment.

Aleutian schools are helping young Unangan students learn about their history and the Unangan language is again being taught. Organisations such as the Aleut Corporation funds language and other cultural programs.

Fisheries

Unangan culture and traditions are today protected and preserved, but new threats to the Unangan do exist. The massive growth of fisheries in the Bering Strait could dramatically reduce local fish stocks. Loss of fish would affect the Unangan way of life, which has depended on ocean resources for thousands of years.

Did you know?
The Unangan received full American citizenship and voting rights in the mid 1960s.

Cultural traditions are being taught to young Unangan students and celebrated at festivals.

Inuit have lived across the Arctic in Greenland and Arctic Canada for more than 1000 years. Some people call Inuit Eskimos. The correct name is Inuit.

The region

The geographic North Pole has one of the coldest climates on Earth, with ice and snow most of the year. Winter lasts for 10 months, from September to June, with an average temperature of minus 40 degrees Celsius. In the summer months of July and August, the average temperature is zero degrees Celsius.

Despite freezing conditions, the Arctic has forests of birch, firs, spruce and mountain ash. The Artic also has **tundra**, growing heath, berries, flowers and grasses.

Population

More than 100 000 Inuit live across a 6000-kilometre Arctic zone from Canada to Greenland. Greenland's population is dominated by more than 50 000 Inuit. Greenland Inuit are citizens of Denmark. The Inuit of Canada are Canadian citizens.

Language

Inuit language is called *Inuktitut*. Inuit also speak the national languages of their countries, such as English in Canada.

Forests in the Arctic need to be able to survive freezing conditions.

Traditional Inuit life

Inuit survived in one of the world's harshest climates by following animal migrations south in winter and north in summer. Husky dog teams pulled **sleds** carrying Inuit and their possessions over the ice. Sled dogs are still used, but most Inuit now live in permanent settlements.

Hunting

On land, Inuit hunted caribou, seals, walrus and birds. At sea, they hunted whales in canoes called kayaks. One whale supplied a village with meat for several months. Whale fat, or blubber, was burned for heating and light.

Housing

Early Inuit housing had driftwood and sod walls dug into the ground. A trapdoor entry prevented cold air from getting in. Villages also had community halls for celebrations and meetings.

Inuit built dome-shaped igloos during hunting expeditions. Igloos were built from bricks cut from the snow.

Clothing

Inuit wore caribou-skin trousers and hooded parkas. Their clothing, called *annuraaq* (say *an-u-rak*) has fur inside and outside for warmth. Boots were of waterproof sealskin.

An Inuit hunter waits at a seal's breathing hole.

Inuit society

Family is at the heart of Inuit society. Traditionally, families shared the work of hunting and gathering, and packing and moving from place to place.

Extended families

Family groups were often made up of three generations, with grandparents and grandchildren all living together. All members of the family were respected equally.

The long winter months were a time of feasting and resting. Often groups of families set up winter villages where they would share resources.

Leaders and elders

Leaders in Inuit society were chosen for their skills and experience. Skilled hunters would be asked to lead hunts, while talented gatherers would lead the berry picking.

Elderly people in Inuit society were respected for their knowledge. The elders told the history and stories of the Inuit. This taught young people about culture, religion, laws, social behaviour, land ownership and hunting.

Did you know?
The Inuit name for shamans is *angakok*. Angakok are believed to have powers to control weather, heal the ill and read the future.

Several generations of Inuit families may live together.

Inuit learning for life

In the past, Inuit children learned from their families and elders.

Learning traditional skills

Young boys learned to hunt. Young girls learned how to fish and where to find berries, roots and grasses.

Traditional Inuit games were played during winter to maintain strength and endurance and improve hunting techniques. One game is the two-foot high kick. Players jump into the air while kicking a target with both legs. The two-foot high kick was the signal that told the village a whale had been caught.

Modern education

Today, like children all over the world, Inuit children go to school. Some schools in Canada and Greenland teach Inuit traditions and culture. Inuit children learn about traditional tools, such as the *aulasautik*, a fishing hook used for ice fishing, and the *qamutik* sled, pulled by dog teams.

The blanket toss is played with a blanket made from walrus hide.

Did you know?

Inuit hunters were thrown into the air from a walrus blanket to see over the horizon during the whaling season. This game, now called the blanket toss, is played during the World Eskimo-Indian Olympics.

Inuit celebrations and rituals

There are many Inuit celebrations throughout the year. One of the most important is the winter *quviasugvik*. Quviasugvik falls near Christmas and has become an Inuit Christmas tradition. The two-week festival is a time for storytelling, drumming, dancing and throat singing.

Canadian Inuit throat singing

The Inuit of Canada play the throat singing game during celebrations. Women face each other and sing from their throats. The winner is the one who can sing the longest.

Birth rituals

In the past, Inuit women moved to a private igloo to give birth. Baby boys were then introduced to families at one month of age, and girls at two months. Shamans name babies when they are eight days old. It is believed names give the babies spiritual protection. Today, most Inuit are born in hospitals.

Death rituals

Today, most Inuit are Christians and follow Christian burials. In the past, Inuit buried their dead under stone markers.

Inuksuk

Important Inuit symbols are large stone markers called *inuksuk*. Inuksuk guide hunters across the ice. Inuksuk are human-shaped, with one arm pointing the way home. An inuksuk is on the Inuit flag.

Throat singers often imitate the sounds of nature.

Did you know?
Inuit elders of Canada's far north still teach throat singing and igloo building.

Inuit arts and crafts

Winter was the time for making art and craft. Inuit women decorated clothes while the men carved bone, wood and stone.

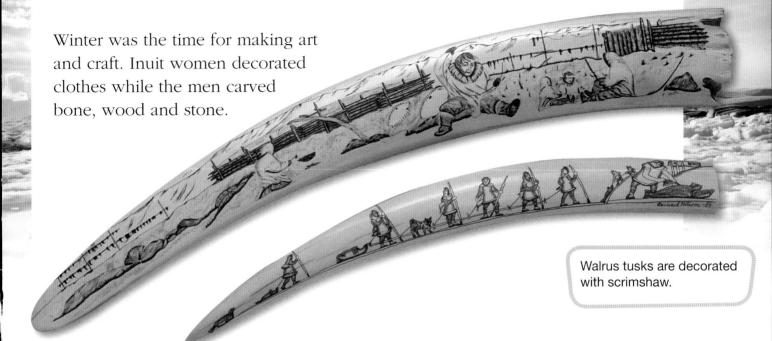

Walrus tusks are decorated with scrimshaw.

Carvings

Inuit are recognised for their artistic carvings, such as *tupilak*. Tupilak are small carvings of naughty spirits made from **narwhal** bone, walrus bone or caribou antler.

Scrimshaw

One of the best known Inuit arts is scrimshaw. Pictures are scratched or carved into ivory or whalebone, then soot from a fire is rubbed over the surface. This makes the carved pictures stand out against the white background. Inuit scrimshaw has been collected by foreigners for centuries.

Embroidery

Inuit women were highly skilled at embroidering clothing and shoes. Fur-lined clothes were heavily decorated, with each family developing their own designs and images.

Inuksuk

Inuit inuksuk are today made as huge sculptures. An inuksuk sculpture has been given to the city of Montreal, in Canada, by the Inuit.

Did you know?

There are many galleries across Greenland and Canada specialising in Inuit arts. These galleries have carvings, wall hangings, scrimshaw, jewellery and basketry.

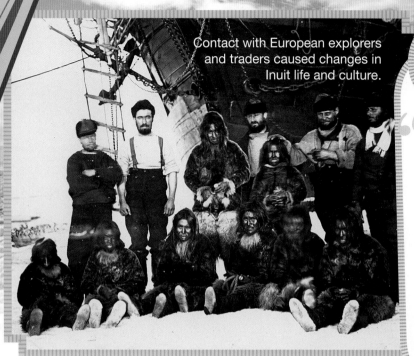
Contact with European explorers and traders caused changes in Inuit life and culture.

Changes to Inuit life

The Inuit lived undisturbed until the late 1500s, after English explorer Martin Frobisher sailed into Arctic waters. When fur traders began exploiting the region, the Inuit way of life changed forever.

The fur trade

During the 1700s, animal skins were in great demand across Europe. Fur hunters and traders arrived in far north Canada and Greenland. In return for Inuit furs, they traded glass beads, iron tools, woollen blankets and other European goods.

The traders brought new diseases such as measles and typhoid. The Inuit had no **immunity** to these diseases and many died.

Lifestyle damaged

Many Inuit began to live in permanent settlements. Their **nomadic** hunting traditions were lost. By the 1960s, this change in lifestyle had severely damaged Inuit communities.

Inuit children were forced into European schools. Children did not learn the skills and culture of their parents and there were fears Inuit culture would be lost.

Inuit survival

During the 1970s, young Inuit studying in boarding schools came together and began fighting for cultural rights. These students began to question the colonisation of Inuit lands.

Land claims

The Inuit push for greater recognition of their cultural and land rights grew. By the 1980s, young Inuit activists were fighting for rights over Inuit territory and to access the earnings from gas and oil mining.

Education today

In Canadian schools, Inuit students are taught the standard curriculum as well as lessons in Inuit culture. Inuit students learn about their history and legends, as well as skills such as how to hunt, build igloos and make traditional clothing. This approach to education is helping preserve the Inuit way of life.

Did you know?

Today, Inuit communities such as Nunavut, in Canada, receive 25 per cent of all mining **royalties**. This helps fund many programs that are building on Inuit cultural foundations.

Learning traditional skills, such as sewing sealskin, connects Inuit people to their culture.

Sami of Sapmi

Sami have lived in the Arctic regions of Norway, Sweden, Finland and Russia for 10 000 years. Fair-skinned Sami people are believed to be related to people from Finland.

There are several different groups of Sami:

- the Northern Sami, the largest group, in northern Finland, Sweden and Norway
- the Southern Sami, in middle Sweden and Norway
- the Eastern Sami, on the Kola Peninsula in Russia.

The region

The area in which the Sami live is called Sapmi. Sapmi winter days are cold, with less than five hours of daylight and an average temperature of minus 30 degrees Celsius.

Summer days have more than 14 hours of daylight, with temperatures averaging between 0 and 5 degrees Celsius.

Population

There are at least 80 000 Sami living across Norway, Sweden and Finland. Around 2000 Sami live in Russia.

Languages

There are many different **dialects** in Sami communities, but most Sami languages are similar. Sami communities also speak the national languages of their countries.

To find out about the Sami flag design: visit http://en.wikipedia.org/wiki/Sami_flag

This Sami family lives in the remote north of Finland.

A Sami girl in traditional clothes pats her family reindeer.

Traditional Sami life

Sami are nomadic reindeer herders, grazing reindeer across the borders of Norway, Sweden, Finland and Russia. Some Sami are also fishermen, living in village settlements.

Food

Sami herd reindeer, sheep and cattle. Sami today are licensed to herd the 750 000 reindeer of the Sapmi region.

Sami **staple foods** are reindeer, fish and sheep. Sami also eat gathered foods such as cloudberries, which are rich in vitamin C.

Meats and fish are dried, salted, smoked and made into sausages to preserve them throughout the year.

Housing

Traditionally, during summer migrations, Sami lived in reindeer-hide tents shaped like teepees. In winter, they lived in dome-shaped houses made from tree branches and **daub**.

Clothing

Traditional Sami clothing made from felt and leather is coloured blue, red and yellow. High-crowned hats are traditionally worn by women. Moccasins and long coats of reindeer skin are also worn.

Did you know?
Reindeer blood is used to make sausages rich in iron.

This Sami woman prepares and sells the furs of foxes that her husband has trapped.

Sami society

Some Sami families are still nomadic reindeer herders. Others live in villages. The Sami have their own government to protect their traditions and rights.

Sami parliaments

In recent years, Sami parliaments have been created in Finland, Sweden and Norway to protect Sami rights and ensure cultural preservation. Reindeer herders' associations also protect Sami rights to herd across nations in the Sapmi region.

Traditional family life

Sami families depend on each other for survival. Sami family units called *siida* are made up of related families.

The oldest family member leads the siida. Leaders decide when to move reindeer foraging grounds and camps. They also discuss issues such as land rights, mining and forestry.

Traditionally, each member of the family has a role to play. Men hunt, trap and herd. Women cure skins, make clothing, preserve meats and gather fruits.

The United Nations says

Indigenous peoples have the right to self-determination. By virtue of that right they freely determine their political status and freely pursue their economic, social and cultural development.

Article 3 of the United Nations Declaration on the Rights of Indigenous Peoples, 2007

Sami learning for life

Sami boys and girls traditionally learn different life skills. Boys are taught to hunt and trap, and herd reindeer, sheep and cattle. Girls are taught to cook, sew, weave and felt.

The first Sami school was opened by **missionaries** in 1632 in Lycksele, Sweden. Sami children were forced to leave their families to attend the school.

Education today

Sami children today go to schools in villages. They learn standard lessons as well as Sami culture. Sami children can now choose to go to schools that teach in their own language.

Nomadic schools

Some Sapmi schools allow nomadic Sami children to attend different schools along the reindeer migration routes. These children are able to learn about their traditional lives with their families and access modern education.

Higher education

Universities in Norway, Sweden and Finland today offer studies in Sami culture, history and language.

Did you know?
Sami children in Russia must study in Russian-language schools.

Sami children learn the Sami language at school in Norway.

Sami celebrations and rituals

In ancient times, the Sun was at the heart of many Sami rituals and poems. Sami believed the Sun was the father and the Earth was the mother.

Christianity

Today, most Sami follow the Lutheran Christian church. They celebrate Christmas and Easter along with other people around the world. These are important Sami festivals.

Easter

Norway's Sami celebrate Easter with sled racing and singing. Forest trees are decorated with candles and ribbons.

Celebrating spring

One of the most important celebrations for the Sami is the annual spring festival. Sami come together to celebrate the end of winter and the new spring growth across the tundra. This time also marks the packing up of winter homes and preparations for the spring and summer reindeer migrations across the four nations.

Did you know?

The word 'tundra', used for the far northern pasture lands, is a Sami word now used all over the world.

Reindeer sled races are part of Sami Easter celebrations in Norway.

26

Traditional Sami clothing is richly decorated with woven and embroidered patterns.

Sami arts and crafts

Sami reindeer herders are nomadic. Their artworks needed to be transportable. Sami arts and crafts are called *duodje*.

Weavings and embroidery

Sami women weave geometric patterns from wool in reds, yellows and blues. Weavings are worn on collars and cuffs of traditional clothing. Women embroider patterns taken from nature onto traditional *kolt* jackets.

Utensils

Bowls, knives and reindeer harnesses are also decorated. Traditional materials included reindeer horn, leather and bone, wood, and iron traded for furs.

Drums, singing and storytelling

Musical Sami arts include *noadi*. Noadi are beautifully carved drums representing the artist's life. Drums were an important part of traditional Sami music making.

Yoiking

Sami have a traditional form of singing called yoiking. Yoiking tells Sami stories, legends and news. Missionaries tried to ban yoiking. They believed it was evil. Today, yoiking is again being practised. Sami musicians are using yoiking in rap, jazz, rock and techno music.

Changes to Sami life

Anthropologists say Sami lived with little interference across Sapmi for at least 10 000 years. They traded animal skins and other goods with southerners, but were left undisturbed.

Colonisation

From the 1600s, people from the south began colonising traditional Sami reindeer feeding grounds. Governments of Sweden, Finland, Russia and Norway introduced taxes on the Sami. Newcomers cleared land and reduced Sami reindeer feeding grounds.

Sami traditional belief systems were affected by missionaries. Some Sami were forced into Christianity.

Mining

In the 1700s, silver and other valuable metals were discovered across Sapmi. Sami people were forced to work for the mines. Their life was severely changed and traditional reindeer foraging routes were lost.

Did you know?

Sami people in Siberia faced great hardship under the **communist** regime of the United Soviet States of Russia. They were forced to relocate to the Kola Peninsula in far north Russia. Today, Russian Sami say they are still **discriminated against**.

The nomadic life of Sami reindeer herders has been threatened by newcomers.

Sami survival

Young Sami people became politically active from the 1970s onwards. By 1986 the Sami national anthem, '*Sami soga lavlla*', was written and the Sami flag created. Land rights for Sami differ across four international boundaries.

Russia

Despite Russian legal protection for the Sami of the Kola Peninsula, Sami lands are still mined, forests logged and reindeer poached. They do not receive royalties or land rehabilitation.

Sweden

Sweden's Government recognised Sami culture in January 2008. Decisions over reindeer herds are today controlled by the Swedish Sami Parliament.

Sami are, however, yet to be granted land rights. They are also banned from their traditional hunting grounds.

Finland

By 2008, Finland had not granted land rights to Sami. The Finnish Sami Parliament has asked Finland to recognise Sami resources in Sapmi.

Norway

Norway's Sami Parliament began in 1989. It protects cultural rights and rights to traditional reindeer grazing lands. Norway has the most advanced Sami land and cultural rights in Sapmi.

The *Sameting*, or Sami Parliament building, in Norway

The future for first peoples of the Arctic

The inhospitable Arctic region gave the Unangan, Inuit and Sami peoples safe haven for thousands of years. They fished the waters and hunted animals. They gathered seasonal fruits and vegetables. In isolation, they created their own religions and understanding of the world. Colonisation forced change to their way of life and beliefs.

Today, there is international recognition of the value of Arctic first peoples' arts, culture and life skills. Governments of the United States, Canada, Russia, Finland, Sweden, Denmark and Norway are attempting to make up for damage to traditional cultures. The United Nations has played a vital role in this turnaround.

Arctic peoples now face a double new threat. Climate change is melting ice and drowning their traditional lands. As the lands are more exposed, the Arctic is more accessible to mining. People of the Arctic are working to reduce the impact of climate change and to ensure they have a voice in the harvesting of Arctic resources, such as oil.

Melting ice is a new threat to the way of life of the indigenous people of the Arctic.

Glossary

amulets symbols worn to protect against evil

anthropologists people who study societies

artefacts items made by humans such as tools and works of art

citizens members of a society with legal protections, rights and responsibilities

colonisation taking over land and establishing a settlement, called a colony

colonists people who have moved from their own country to live in a new settlement in another country, called a colony

commercial fisheries very large fishing companies

communist a political system where there is no private property and the community owns everything, with the aim of achieving equality

culture the traditions of a people

daub mud or clay spread over a surface to make a wall

dialects variations of a language spoken in a particular area

discriminated against treated differently because they belong to a particular category, such as race, religion or gender

dispossession the taking of land or property from its owners

driftwood wood found washed up on beaches

elders people who are respected and influential because of their age and experience

geometric patterns patterns of regular lines and shapes

immunity the ability to resist or recover from disease

indigenous people the first people to live in a region

migrated moved from one place to another

missionaries people who work in another country to spread their religious faith

narwhal small, white species of whale found in the Arctic

nomadic people who frequently move from place to place

resources the natural products of an area, such as water, food and minerals

rituals special ways of doing things, often part of religious ceremonies

royalties money paid to a landowner in return for the right to harvest or mine resources

sinew strong string-like material that attaches muscle to bone

sleds whalebone or wooden carts that slide across ice and snow

staple foods the main types of food that are eaten daily

sustainably living in a way that does not use up natural resources

tundra vast, treeless marshy lands in the Arctic Circle

United Nations an international organisation of countries that promotes peace and cooperation

Index